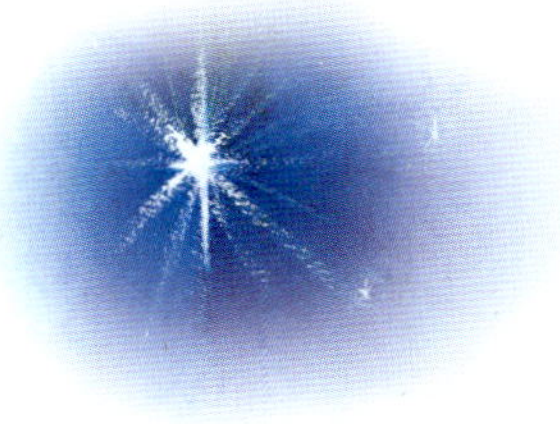

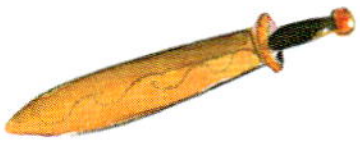

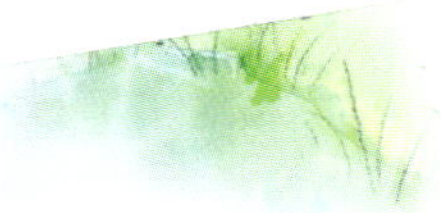

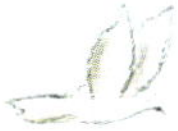

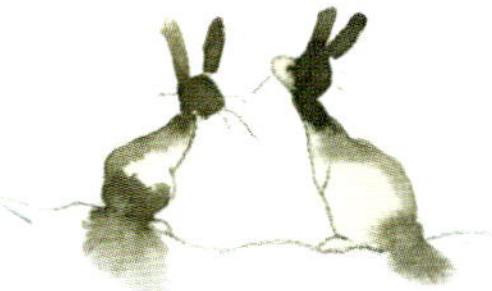

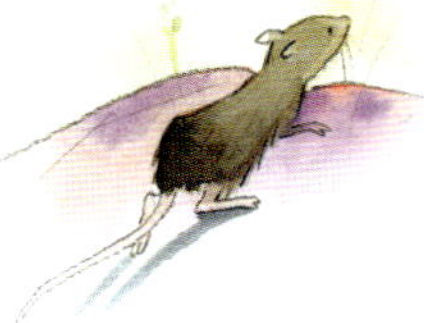

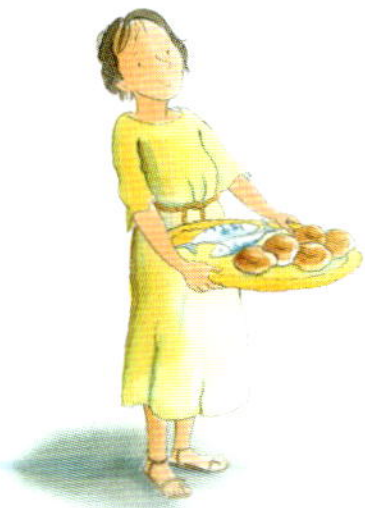

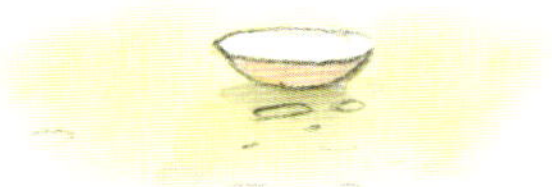

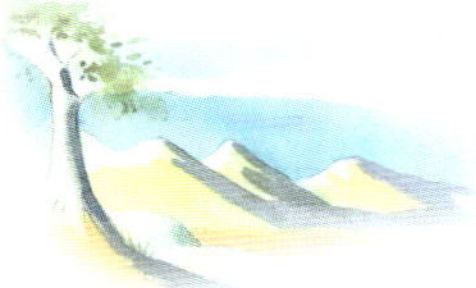

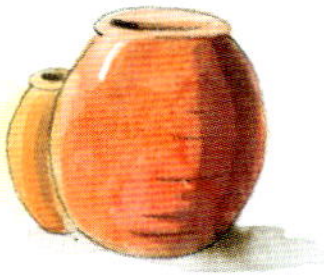

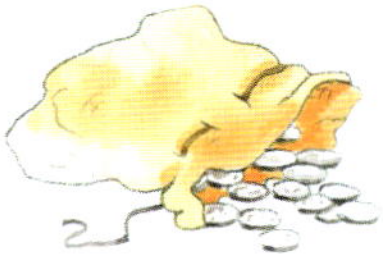

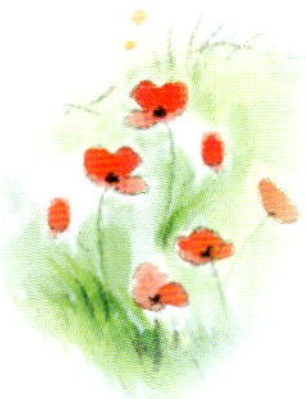

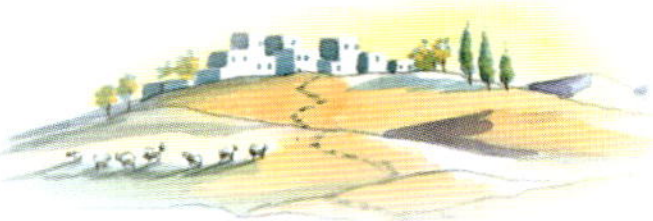

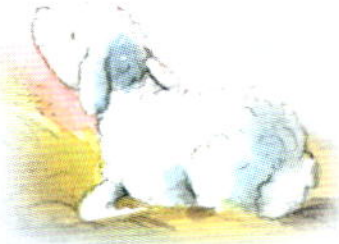

First edition 2011

Copyright © 2011 Anno Domini Publishing
www.ad-publishing.com
Text copyright © 2011 Marion Thomas
Illustrations copyright © 2011 Frank Endersby

All rights reserved

Published 2014 by Authentic Media Limited
52, Presley Way, Crownhill,
Milton Keynes, MK8 0ES, UK.

Conforms to EN71 and AS/NZS ISO 8124

Printed and bound in China

A Child's Life of Jesus

Marion Thomas and Frank Endersby

Contents

8	The Angel Gabriel
10	The Journey to Bethlehem
12	No Room at the Inn
14	Some Very Frightened Shepherds
16	Wise Men from the East
18	The Escape into Egypt
20	Jesus in Jerusalem
22	John Baptizes Jesus
24	Time in the Desert
26	Fishermen Friends
28	A New Way to Live
30	The Man Who Couldn't Walk
32	The Soldier Who Believed
34	Who is Jesus?
36	Jairus' Little Girl
38	Food for a Hungry Crowd
40	Jesus Heals a Deaf Man
42	The Story of the Good Samaritan
44	The Story of the Lost Sheep
46	The Story of the Loving Father
48	Treasure in Heaven
50	Ten Men with Leprosy

52	The Best Way to Pray
54	Jesus Blesses Children
56	The Man who Had Too Much
58	A Very Special Gift
60	Blind Bartimaeus Sees
62	Jesus Makes a New Friend
64	Mary, Martha and Lazarus
66	Jesus rides into Jerusalem
68	Robbers in the Temple
70	Living God's Way
72	Jesus the Servant
74	Thirty Pieces of Silver
76	Soldiers in the Garden
78	Peter is Ashamed
80	The Crown of Thorns
82	The Three Crosses
84	Jesus is Buried
86	The Empty Tomb
88	Thomas Believes
90	Breakfast by the Lake
92	Jesus Returns to Heaven

The Angel Gabriel
Luke 1:26-38

Jesus was not born into an ordinary family. It all began very strangely with the visit of an angel.

'Hello, Mary,' said the angel Gabriel. 'God thinks you are very special.' Mary was so shocked at an angel appearing in her home that she felt quite faint. 'Don't be afraid,' Gabriel went on. 'This is very good news. God will bless you with a baby son. When he is born, you will name him Jesus. Everyone will be amazed at the things he does, and people will know that he is God's Son. He will be king over God's people for ever.'

Finally Mary found her voice. 'But how can I have a baby? I don't even have a husband yet,' she said.

'Nothing is impossible with God,' Gabriel replied. 'The Holy Spirit will make this happen. Jesus will be the Son of God himself.'

Mary loved God. She trusted him.

'I am God's servant,' she said.

9

The Journey to Bethlehem
Luke 2:1-5

Mary had been engaged to Joseph, the carpenter, for some time. When she told him that she was expecting a baby and all that the angel had told her, Joseph was sad. He loved Mary, but he did not think an angel had visited her – things like that just didn't happen…

Then one night, it did happen! The angel Gabriel spoke to Joseph in a dream, and told him that God wanted him to marry Mary and take care of the baby who would be God's Son.

Months passed and Mary's pregnancy showed in her round belly. She became tired and knew that soon her baby would be born. Around that time the Roman emperor made it clear that he wanted to count all the people in the lands he ruled over so he could tax them. They had to return to the town of their ancestors for a census.

So Mary and Joseph went to Bethlehem because Joseph was descended from King David. It was a long way for a pregnant woman to walk.

12

No Room at the Inn
Luke 2:6-7

There was noise and bustle everywhere when Mary and Joseph arrived in Bethlehem. They were not the only visitors. There were soldiers and families and animals, and more people looking for somewhere to stay than there were places to put them.

Joseph found a place where they could shelter for the night. They shared it with the animals that were kept there, but Mary knew her baby would wait no longer. Not long afterwards, the cries of her tiny baby son mixed with the sounds of night-time in Bethlehem. Mary remembered what the angel Gabriel had said.

'Jesus,' she whispered. 'Your name is Jesus.'

Mary wrapped up her baby warmly and made a bed for him in the manger, filled with hay.

Some Very Frightened Shepherds
Luke 2:8-20

Shepherds watched over their sheep at night to protect them from wild animals. Now, outside Bethlehem, a group of them were warming their hands and settling for the night.

Suddenly the sky was filled with bright light and as they fell back in fear, they heard the voice of the angel Gabriel.

'Don't be afraid!' said Gabriel. 'I have some wonderful news for you and for everyone on earth! A baby has been born today. No ordinary baby, but the one you have been promised, the one you have been waiting for – your Saviour. You will know him when you find him because he is wrapped in cloths and lying in a manger.'

Before the shepherds had taken in his message, he was joined by hundreds, thousands of angels, all singing praises to God.

'Glory to God in highest heaven, and peace to his people on earth!'

Then the angels left the shepherds alone, with the sound of their singing ringing in their ears.

'Well – what are we waiting for?' said one.

The shepherds found the baby, who was lying in the manger, just as the angels had said. Then they told everyone they saw about what had happened that night.

Wise Men from the East
Matthew 2:1-12

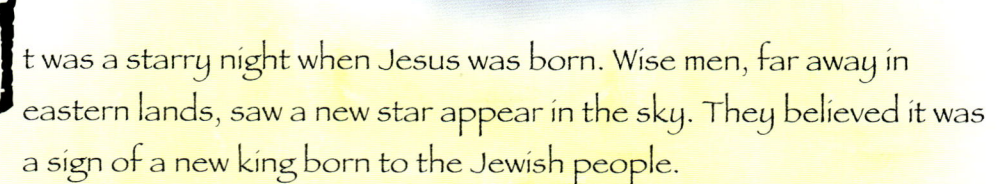

It was a starry night when Jesus was born. Wise men, far away in eastern lands, saw a new star appear in the sky. They believed it was a sign of a new king born to the Jewish people.

They packed gifts, prepared for a long journey and travelled by night, following the star.

When the men neared Jerusalem, they went to the palace of King Herod, assuming they would find a baby king there. But Herod was suspicious, then anxious – then angry – at the thought that there might be a king to replace him. He thought of a plan to remove the baby king – as soon as the men from the east had found him.

'Try Bethlehem,' Herod said. 'But do come back and tell me when you find him, so that I can worship him too.'

The men followed the star to Bethlehem where they found Jesus, in a house with his mother Mary. They offered him their gifts

– gold, frankincense and myrrh – and bowing low, they worshipped him.

Mary watched thoughtfully as the men left to return to their own country. What could all this mean?

The Escape into Egypt
Matthew 2:13-23

Joseph slept badly that night. Then he woke suddenly. An angel had warned him in a dream that Mary's son was in danger. King Herod would not rest until the child was dead.

Joseph woke Mary and together they gathered their things. They took Jesus by night on a long journey into Egypt.

Meanwhile King Herod was furious. He knew that the men from the east must have found the child and gone back another way. In his rage he sent soldiers to kill all the little boys under two years old – a time he had worked out from what the men had told him.

Jesus spent his early years in Egypt. When at last Herod died, an angel told Joseph that it was safe to return to their home country. Joseph took Mary and Jesus back to live in Nazareth in Galilee and they made their home there.

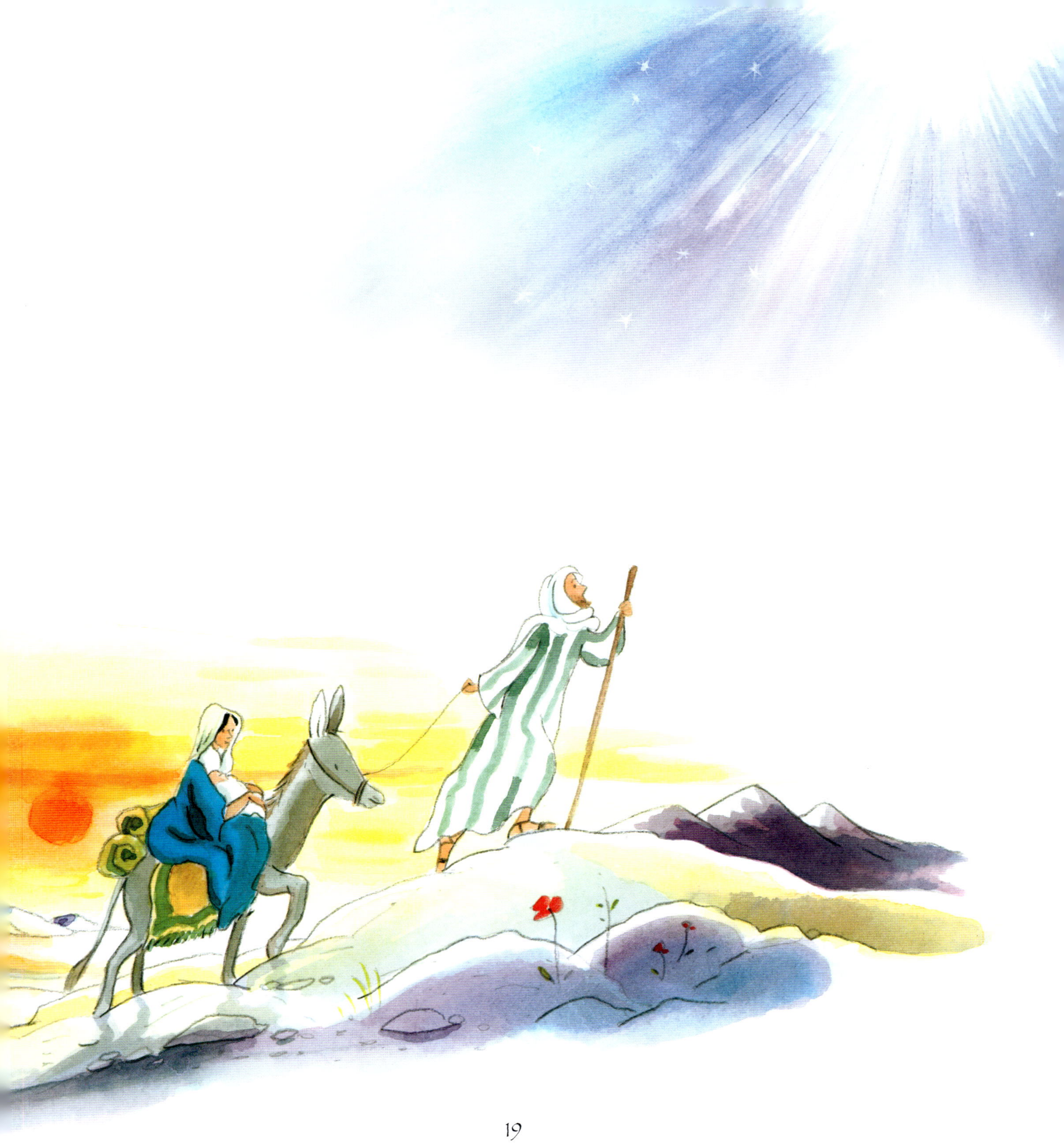

Jesus in Jerusalem
Luke 2:41-52

The years passed. Now it was the time that Jesus looked forward to every year, because everyone was going to celebrate the feast of the Passover in Jerusalem. Families and friends travelled together on the pilgrimage that took them from little Nazareth to the busy bustling city. And this was the year that Jesus was twelve.

Everything went well until the return journey when, after walking all day, Mary and Joseph couldn't find Jesus. At first Mary thought that Jesus was with the other children. But soon they found that he was nowhere to be seen. Anxiously they made their way back to Jerusalem, leaving their friends behind.

Where could Jesus be? To their surprise, Mary and Joseph found Jesus, perfectly well, sitting, talking with the teachers in the temple.

'We have been so worried!' Mary said to Jesus. 'How could you do this?'

'Why were you looking for me?' said Jesus, equally surprised. 'Surely you knew I needed to be here, in my Father's house?'

Mary and Joseph looked at each other and shook their heads. They didn't understand what he meant. Jesus went back with them to Nazareth. But Mary quietly stored all this in her heart.

John Baptizes Jesus
Luke 3:3-22

Elizabeth was one of Mary's relatives. Her son, John, had grown up around the same time as Jesus. Now John was a grown man and he spent his time in the desert, living apart from other people. He lived on a diet of wild honey and locusts.

John travelled from place to place giving people a message from God.

'Repent!' John told anyone who would listen. 'Tell God you are sorry for all the bad things you have done. Ask God to forgive you and then change your ways. Be kind to others, be generous to the poor, be fair in everything you do.'

Then John encouraged them to be baptized in the River Jordan as a sign that their sins had been washed away.

One day, Jesus came to the river and asked John to baptize him. John knew that Jesus had not done any bad things. He didn't need to be baptized.

'I want to do this, John,' said Jesus. 'Please baptize me.'

As Jesus came up out of the water, he saw a dove above him and everyone there heard someone say: 'You are my Son whom I love very much. I am very pleased with you.' God had spoken.

Time in the Desert
Luke 4:1-13

Jesus was around thirty years old. It was time for him to start the work that God wanted him to do. First he spent some time in the desert, thinking and praying. During this time he had nothing to eat for forty days. Jesus was very hungry.

'If you are God's son, make these stones into bread to eat,' said the devil.

'The scriptures tell us that man needs more than bread to live,' Jesus replied.

The devil then took Jesus to a very high place. 'Worship me, and I will give you all the kingdoms of the world,' he said.

'The scriptures tell us that we should worship God, and no one else,' replied Jesus.

The devil then took Jesus to the top of the temple. 'Throw yourself down! The scriptures tell us that God will send angels to catch you,' he said.

'The scriptures also say that we should not put God to the test,' replied Jesus.

The devil knew who Jesus was – and he had tested him. But Jesus had not given in.

Fishermen Friends
Luke 5:1-11

Jesus started to talk to people about how much God loved them. They crowded around him, wanting to hear more, near Lake Galilee.

'Can you push your boat out a little so I can talk to people from there?' Jesus asked Peter. Peter was washing his nets with his brother Andrew. Then Jesus talked to the people from Peter's boat. Afterwards Jesus asked to be taken further out into deeper water. 'Let down your nets and do some fishing,' Jesus suggested.

'I'll do it,' Peter told him, 'but we fished all night and caught nothing.'

As soon as they put their nets into the water, they were filled with silvery, slithering fish – so many that the nets couldn't hold them. James and John came to help them but the catch was so heavy that both boats started to sink. Peter looked at the fish then at Jesus – he couldn't believe what had just happened.

'From now on,' said Jesus, 'I want you to follow me and catch men instead of fish.'

Peter, Andrew, James and John left their nets from that moment. They became the first of twelve men who followed Jesus.

27

A New Way to Live
Matthew 5:21-25, 38-48; 6:1-4, 25-34

Jesus taught his new friends, his disciples, how to follow God's ways. He explained the laws that Moses had given them long ago, so that they began to understand how God wanted them to live.

'You know that you must not murder,' Jesus said. 'But when you hate someone, or wish that bad things will happen to them – that's just as bad. Learn to love your enemies and be kind to people who hurt you. Forgive people who have been unkind to you and make peace with them. Only by doing this will you be different from people who don't know about God's love.

'Give generously to anyone who needs your help but do it quietly and secretly. Treat other people kindly – think about what you would want, and do that for them.

'And don't worry so much. Trust God to give you enough to eat and clothes to wear. He cares about you even more than these birds and flowers around you. And look at them! The birds have enough to eat and the flowers are beautiful. Do what is right and good and kind, and God will take good care of you.'

The Man Who Couldn't Walk

Luke 5:18-26

Four men had heard all about what Jesus said and did. They had a friend who could not walk. He couldn't even sit up. Maybe Jesus would make him well.

So when Jesus was in Capernaum, they carried their friend to see him. But they were not the only people who wanted to see Jesus. The teachers of the law of Moses were talking to him about the things he said about God. There was no room for them inside the house with their stretcher.

They looked at the steps outside leading to the roof of the house. Then carefully the four friends made their way up the steps and began to make a hole in the mud and branches that made up the roof. The people below stared up at them. Jesus smiled up at them.

When the hole was big enough, they lowered their friend down into the room. Jesus knew they believed he could make the man well.

'It's time to go home,' Jesus said to the man. 'Stand up and take your bed away with you.'

The people there gasped as the man stood up. Jesus had healed him, just as his friends had hoped. But the teachers of the law frowned and shook their heads.

The Soldier Who Believed
Matthew 8:5-13

Some people feared the Romans who lived in their towns. Others hated them. But in Capernaum there was a Roman soldier in charge of many men. He loved God and had paid for the synagogue to be built in Capernaum. People liked him and respected him.

One day he came to Jesus. There was something wrong.

'Please,' he said to Jesus, 'I need your help. My servant is ill and in terrible pain.'

'Of course,' replied Jesus. 'I will come straight away and heal him.'

'There's no need,' said the soldier. 'I don't want to bother you to come to my house. Just say the word and I know he will be healed. I command many men and they do as I tell them. It's the same for you – speak and it will be done.'

Jesus turned to his friends, surprised.

'There are many people here who love God and have known him since they were children – but even they do not have such faith. I have never met anyone who trusts God as this man does.'

Then Jesus told the soldier that his servant was healed. When the soldier returned to his house, he found his servant well again, just as Jesus had promised.

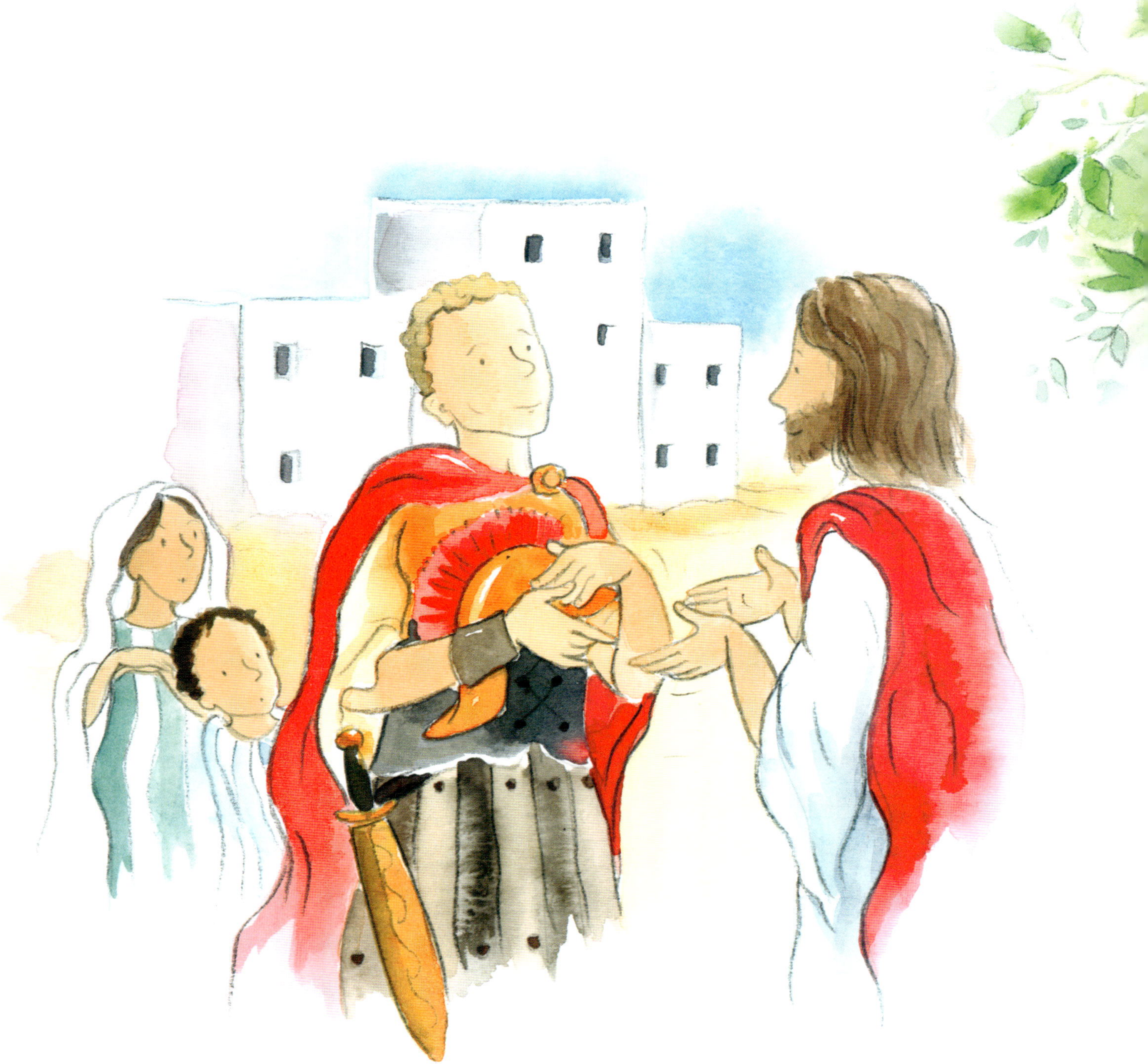

Who is Jesus?
Luke 8:22-25

Jesus was tired. He had been surrounded by people all day long and many had gone away happy and healed from their illnesses. Now Jesus needed some time to rest and be alone for a while.

His friends started to sail the boat to the other side of Lake Galilee. Within minutes, Jesus was asleep.

Suddenly, clouds covered the sun and, from nowhere, a storm blew up over the lake. Choppy waves pushed water into the fishing boat.

'Master! Help us – or we'll drown!' they shouted.

Jesus woke up and saw the frightened faces of his friends.

'Peace. Be still,' he said to the wind and the waves.

Almost as suddenly as it had started, the storm died down. Soon the waves were once more gentle ripples on the water.

The men looked at each other, amazed. Who could this be? Who was their friend, the man who spoke to the wind and waves and calmed a storm?

Jairus' Little Girl
Luke 8:40-55

Jesus was met by a crowd of people when he came back across the lake. Jairus made his way through the people looking very anxious.

'Please come quickly!' he said to Jesus. 'It's my little girl. She's dying!'

Jesus followed Jairus as fast as the crowd would allow. But suddenly he stopped.

'Who touched me?' he asked looking around him.

There were people all around. Surely they were all touching him! But a woman came forward, her eyes cast down.

'It was me,' she whispered. 'I knew if I could just touch your cloak, I would be healed.'

'Go in peace,' said Jesus. 'You are healed because you trusted me.'

But it was too late for Jairus' little girl. A man came from his house to say that she had died. Jesus would not listen. He encouraged Jairus to carry on and together they went into the house with Peter, James and John.

'Get up, little girl,' Jesus said to the figure on the bed. The girl opened her eyes and smiled at her parents. 'I think she's hungry,' Jesus said. Her parents cried with happiness. Jesus had healed their little girl.

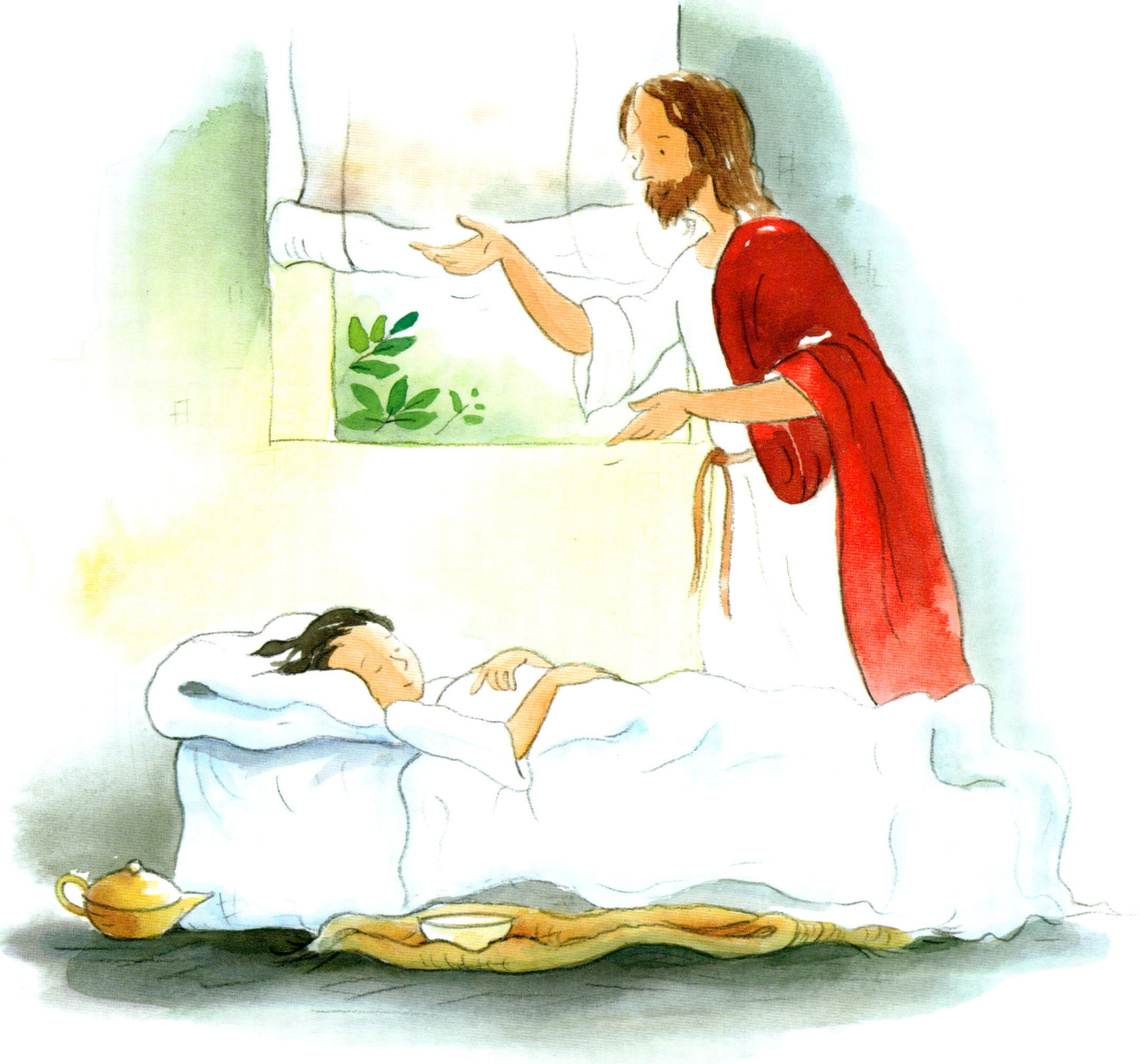

Food for a Hungry Crowd
John 6:1-13

Jesus had been teaching the people about God and healing those who were ill all day. They were all far from home – far from anywhere where they could get something to eat.

'Where can we buy bread for all these people?' Jesus asked. Philip could hardly believe what Jesus had asked. There were more than 5,000 people there! But Andrew came forward with a young boy.

'This boy has offered us five pieces of bread and two little fish,' he said to Jesus. 'But it won't go very far!'

'Don't worry,' Jesus smiled at the boy. He took the food. 'Now, let's get everyone sitting down on the grass.'

Jesus thanked God for the food and broke the bread and fish into pieces so it could be shared. Everyone shared with everyone else. Everyone had enough to eat – and twelve baskets full of leftovers were collected. The people who were nearest to Jesus knew that what had happened was a miracle. Jesus had provided food for thousands of people – with only a boy's packed lunch.

Jesus Heals a Deaf Man

Mark 7:31-37

As people heard about all the things that Jesus did, they looked out for him, hoping he would help them too.

One day some people brought a man to Jesus who could not hear, and because he could not hear, he had never learned to speak.

'Please, can you help him?' they asked Jesus. 'Can you make him well?'

Jesus touched the man's ears and tongue. Then he said 'Be opened!'

Suddenly the man looked at Jesus and then he looked all around him, surprised. He could hear the birds singing. He could hear the sounds of the wind in the trees and the waves on the pebbles by the Sea of Galilee. He could hear the voices of his friends talking not far away. He was also able to speak.

Jesus had healed the deaf man – and people could not stop talking about it.

The Story of the Good Samaritan
Luke 10:25-37

Jesus loved to talk about God and people loved to listen. Sometimes they asked him questions. Often he answered them by telling a story.

'I know I must love God and my neighbour too,' a man said to Jesus one day. 'But tell me who my neighbour is.'

'There was a man travelling on the long and lonely road from Jerusalem to Jericho,' Jesus said. 'Robbers jumped out and attacked him, stealing everything he had and leaving him lying at the side of the road, badly hurt.

'First a priest walked past him, then a Levite. Both were too religious and busy to stop and help. They pretended they couldn't see the man who needed them.

'But the Samaritan who walked along that long and lonely road was not too religious and was not too busy. He stopped and gave the man water to drink. He bathed his wounds and helped him onto his own donkey. Then he took him to an inn and paid for a clean bed so the man could rest there till he was better.

'Take good care of him,' the Samaritan said. 'When I come back this way, I will pay for anything more you have spent on his care.'

'So tell me,' Jesus asked the man, 'who do you think was a good neighbour to the man who was hurt? You need to make sure you act in the same way that he did.'

43

The Story of the Lost Sheep
Luke 15:4-7

All sorts of people came to listen to Jesus. They weren't all good people. Some were the tax collectors, hated by everyone. Many thought they didn't deserve God's love. Most were just ordinary people.

Jesus welcomed them all. But the church leaders who kept all the rules – the Pharisees from the temple and the religious teachers – couldn't understand why Jesus would want to be their friend.

So Jesus asked them a question.

'Imagine you are a farmer who owns a hundred sheep. One day you count only ninety-nine. What would you do? Would you sit back and be happy that you still have ninety-nine sheep? Or would you be worried about the one that was lost and alone? I'll tell you what you would do! You would leave the other sheep safe in their fold and not rest until you have found the one that was lost. Then you would be so happy that you would bring him home and tell all your friends.

'Imagine what it's like for God. There is great joy in heaven over just one person who is sorry and asks God to forgive them.'

45

The Story of the Loving Father
Luke 15:11-24

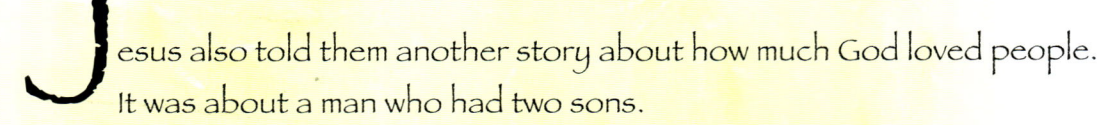

Jesus also told them another story about how much God loved people. It was about a man who had two sons.

'"Father," said the younger son, "I want you to give me my inheritance now – before you die. I want to travel and see the world."

'So the father gave his son a large sum of money. He watched sadly as his son packed his bags and went away. The boy travelled and made friends. He spent his inheritance enjoying himself and everything seemed fine – until he found that he had spent everything he had. Then a famine swept through the country. The boy was so hungry that he had to find work. So the boy who had so much now had a job taking care of pigs. And he was still hungry.

'Then the boy realized how silly he was. He thought about his father and all the people who worked for him. He knew they all had plenty to eat. "I will go home to my father," he thought, "and tell him how sorry I am. I don't deserve to be called his son, but perhaps he will let me work for him."

'So the boy went home. But his father had been waiting for him. He ran towards him and threw his arms around him. "Father, I am so sorry…" the boy began. But the father had already forgiven him. He was already calling his servants to find clean clothes for his son and prepare a feast for him. "Look! My son has come back," he told them all. "I thought he was lost – but now he's found! Let's celebrate!"'

Treasure in Heaven
Luke 12:13-33

Jesus talked about God's love – but he also talked about money.

'It's easy to think money can solve all your problems – but be careful! Money is not everything and greed can spoil your life.

'Once there was a rich farmer who had a very good harvest: his barns were overflowing with all that he had grown. He decided to pull them down and build big, new buildings. He was very pleased with all his money and everything he owned – and he thought he would now retire and enjoy it all.

'But that night was his last on earth. He died before he could enjoy any of it. He had put all his effort into making money – but he couldn't take it with him.

'Don't make the same mistake,' said Jesus. 'People are more important than things. Do good things. Be kind and honest. If you share what you have with those who need it, it will be like storing up treasure in heaven. Then no one can steal it away and no moths can eat it. That's the way to live your life.'

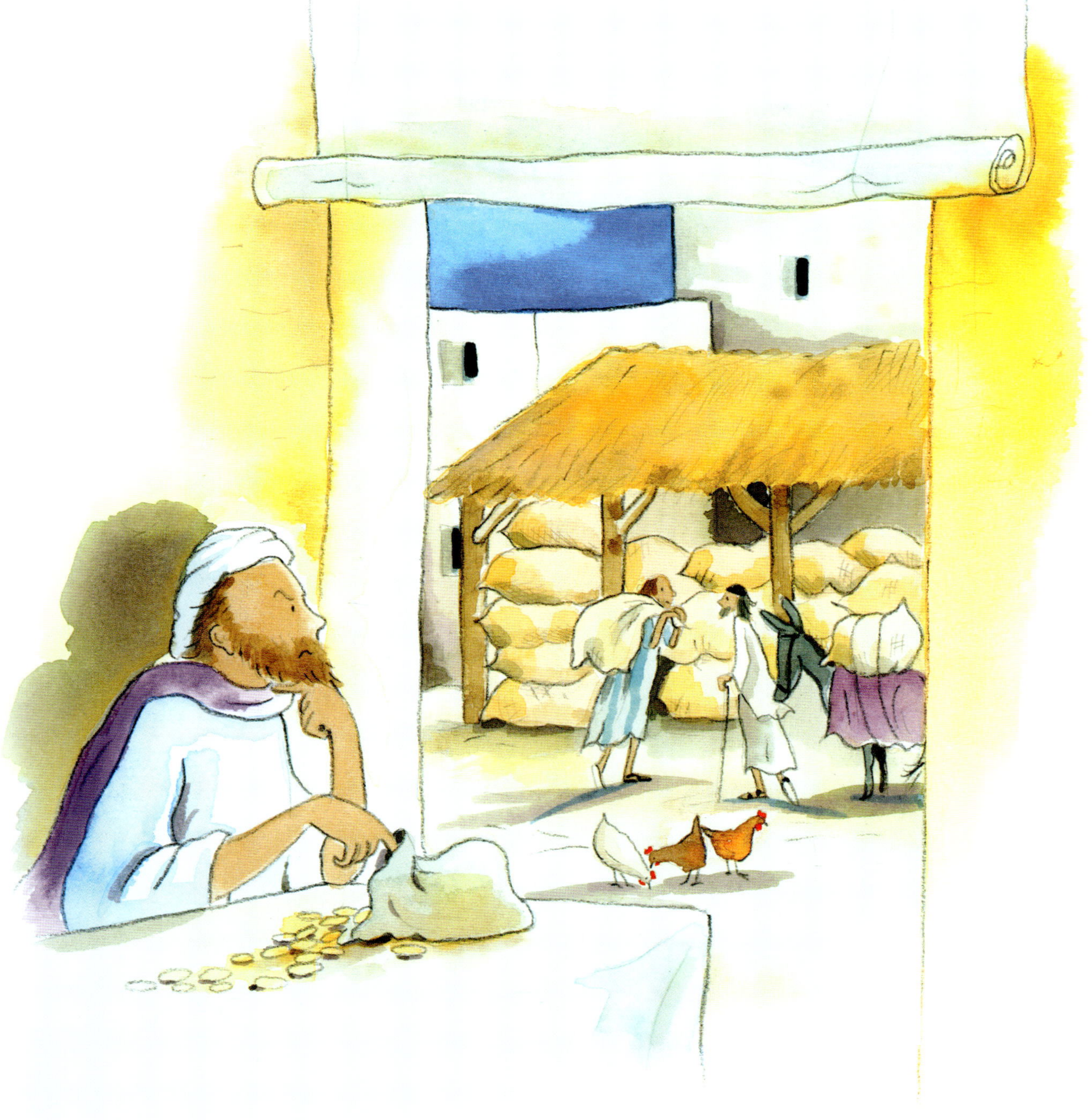

Ten Men with Leprosy
Luke 17:11-19

Most people would keep their distance if they saw lepers nearby. They were afraid of the skin disease that damaged their fingers and toes and noses. So lepers had to live somewhere else. They couldn't live with their families any more.

But Jesus was not like other people. As he travelled towards Jerusalem, Jesus reached a village where he saw ten men huddled together. They knew who he was.

'Jesus, please! Help us, if you will!'

Jesus came closer.

'Of course I will help you,' he said. 'Go and see your priests. You are healed. You can return to your homes.'

The men were very happy as they realized that Jesus had healed them. One man, a Samaritan, came back to Jesus, a big smile on his face.

'Thank you!' the man said. 'You have changed my life!'

'But where are the others?' said Jesus. 'Are they not happy too?'

The Best Way to Pray
Luke 18:9-14

Jesus often spent time talking to God. He knew God was his father. He knew God wanted to spend time with him.

'Let me tell you a story about prayer,' Jesus said one day.

'Two men went into the temple. They both wanted to pray. The first man stood where everyone could see him. He prayed in a loud voice so everyone could hear what he said. "Thank you, Lord, that I am not greedy. Thank you that I am good and kind, honest and generous. Thank you that I am not like that man over there!"

'The other man was on his knees. He whispered to God so no one else could hear him. "Please forgive me, Lord. I am so sorry for all the bad things I have done."

'Both men prayed,' said Jesus. 'God listened to both of them. But God was able to help the man who needed him and that man went away at peace. Make sure your prayers are like his. The other man only wanted to tell God (and other people) how good he was.'

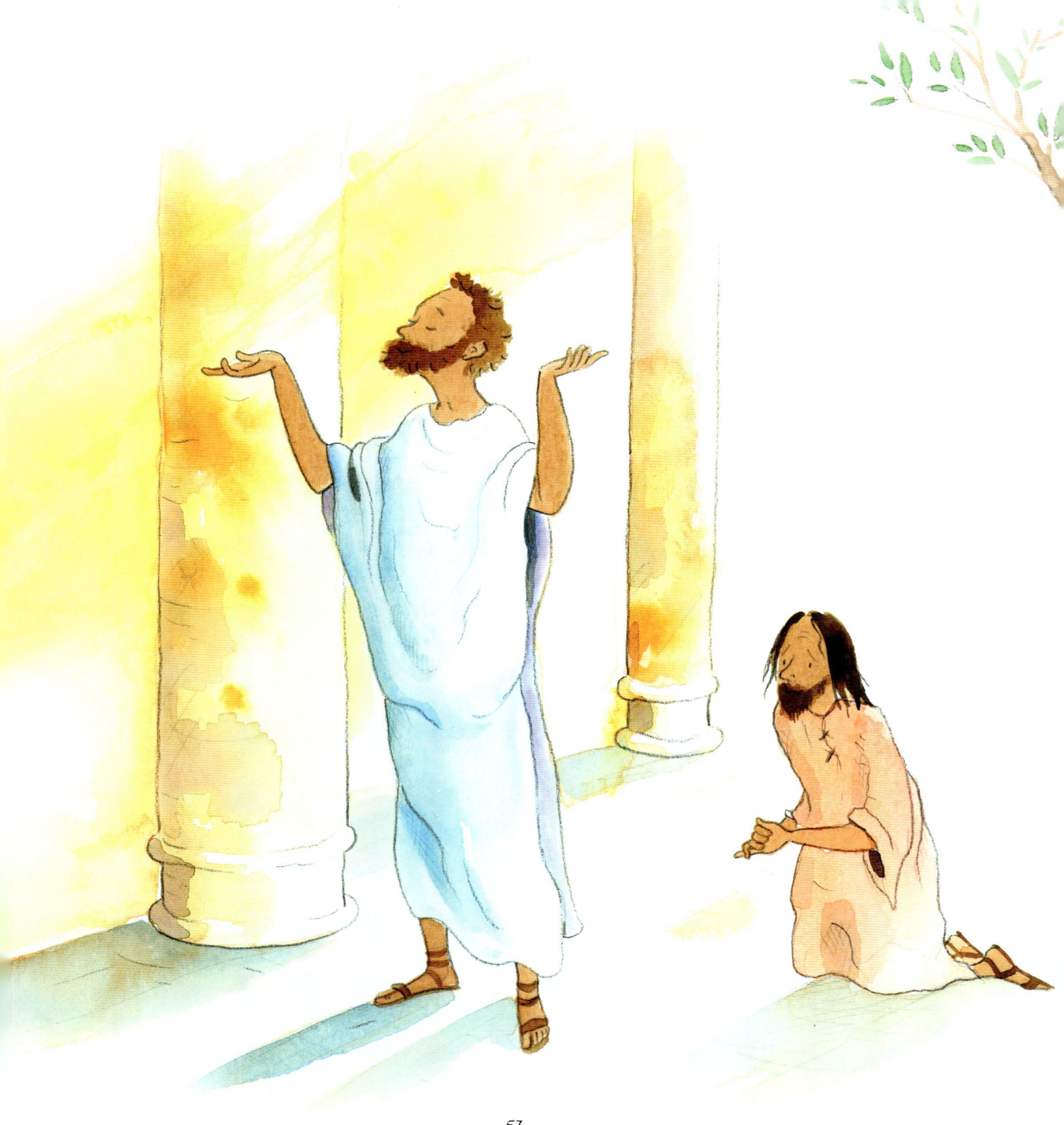

Jesus Blesses Children
Luke 18:15-17

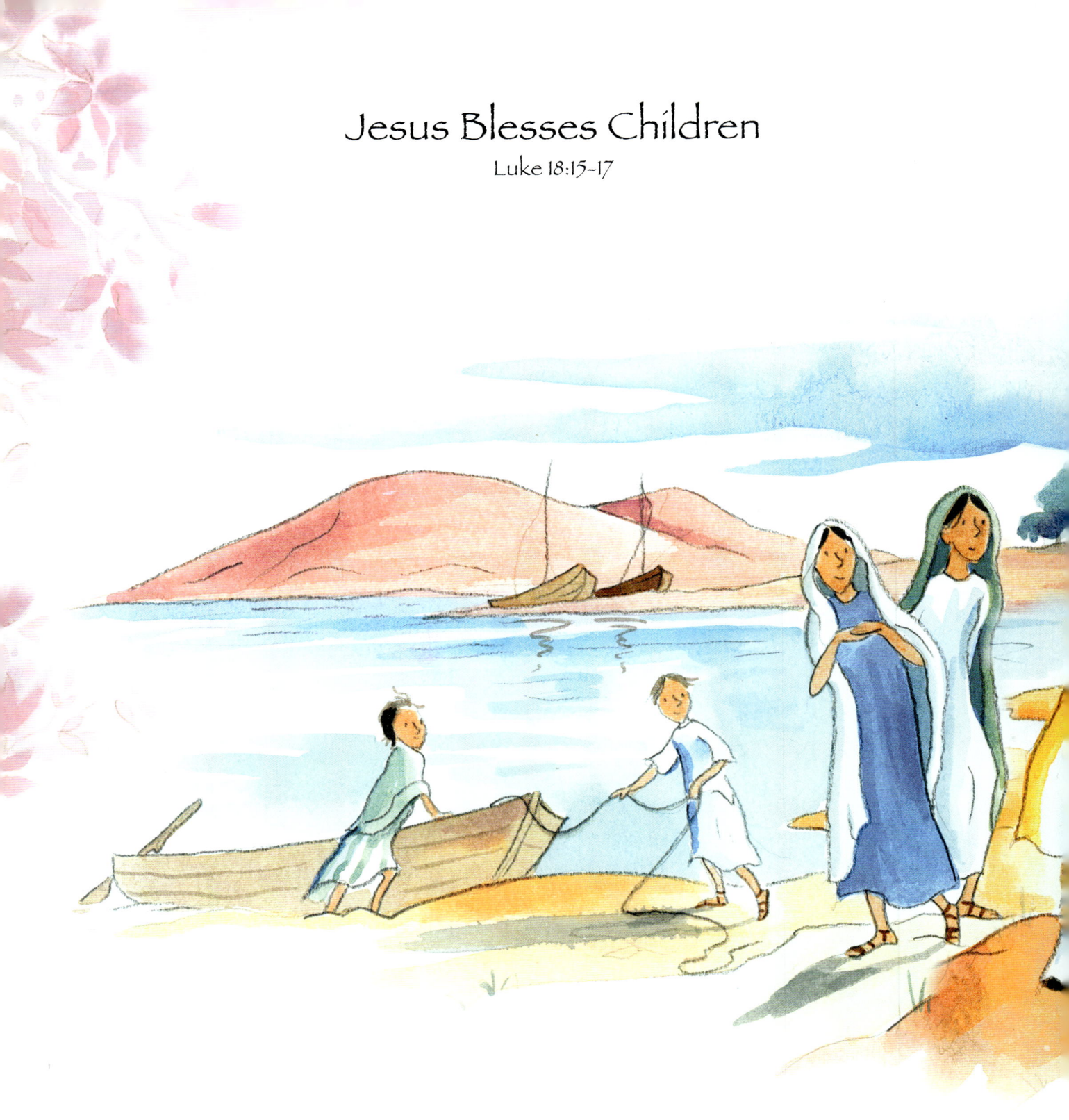

'Look, there's Jesus!' said a mother to her child. 'Shall we go and see him?'

Other mothers, other children followed. They all wanted Jesus to bless their child. Jesus always had time for the children, even if he was busy, even if he was tired.

Sometimes his friends tried to keep them away. They thought he had more important things to do.

'Let the children come to me. Don't ever try to stop them,' said Jesus. 'God's kingdom will be full of people like them. No one can come to God unless they are like these children – ready to trust him because they know he loves them.'

The Man Who had Too Much
Luke 18:18-30

One day a rich young man came to Jesus for help.

'Tell me,' the man said, 'what must I do to live with God in heaven?'

Jesus smiled at him. 'I am sure you know all the commandments that Moses taught? You need to obey them.'

'I know them,' the man replied. 'I have always done my best to follow them.'

'Good. Now, go and sell everything you have. Give the money to people who need it more than you do. Then come and join my friends. Follow me.'

The young man suddenly looked awkward. This wasn't the answer he had expected. He wasn't sure he could do it. He was rich and didn't want to give away the things that mattered to him. The young man shook his head and went away sadly.

'It is easier for a camel to walk through the eye of a needle than for a rich man to enter God's kingdom,' Jesus said.

'We left everything to follow you,' said Peter.

'I know,' Jesus replied. 'And you will all be rewarded. Put God first and nothing else seems important. God will make sure you have all you need.'

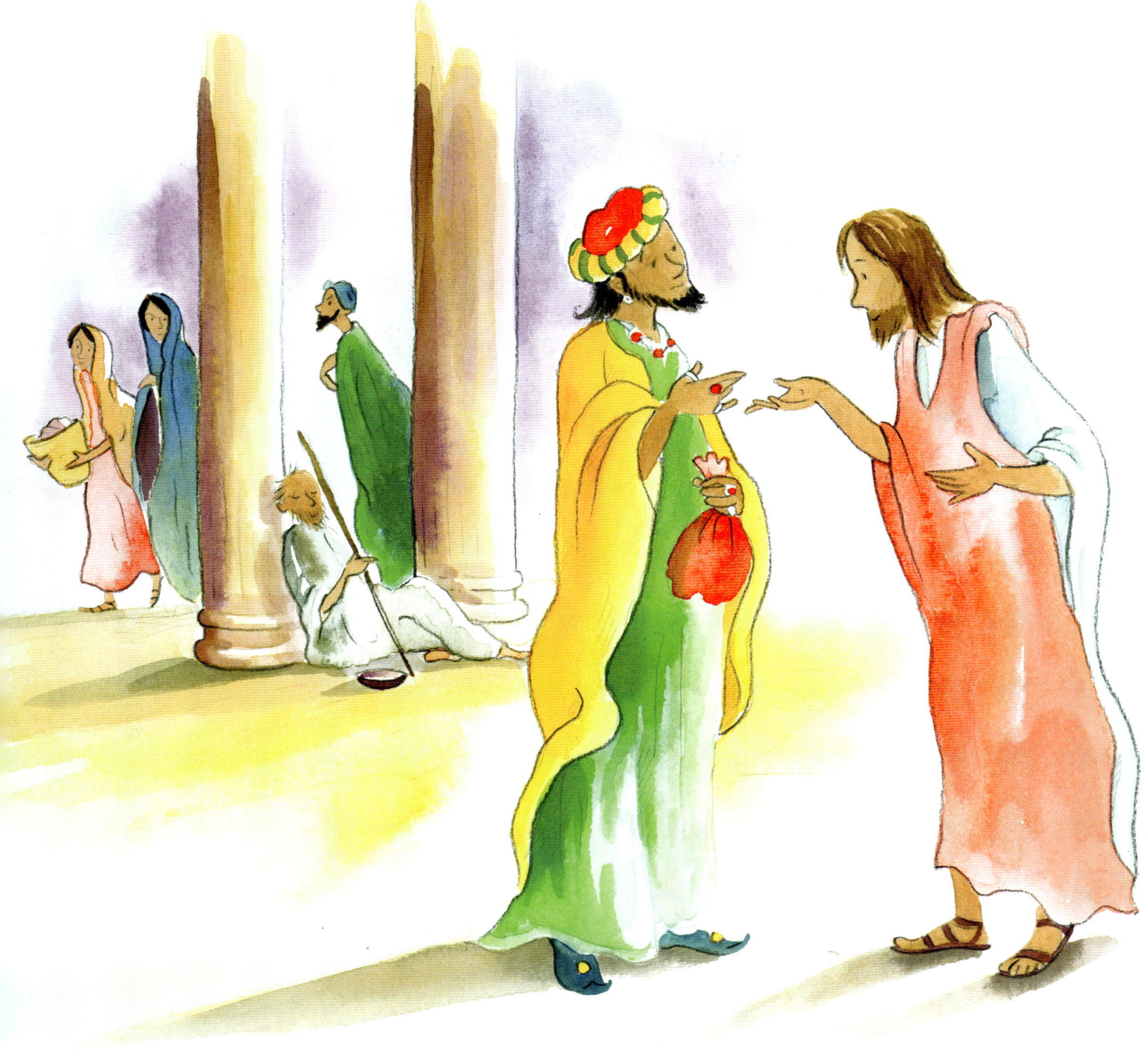

58

A Very Special Gift
Mark 14:3-11

Jesus had been invited to Simon's house for supper. The men were talking and eating together.

But then everyone went quiet. A woman came into the room carrying a small jar. She came closer to Jesus and, without saying anything, she opened the jar and poured some perfume over his head. The smell was beautiful. The perfume must have been very expensive.

Simon and his friends watched. They couldn't believe what they were seeing.

'What are you doing?' said one of Jesus' friends. 'This is a terrible waste. We could have sold this perfume and given the money to the poor!'

'No, not this time,' said Jesus quietly. 'She has given me a very special gift. You can help the poor any time you choose. But I will not be here much longer. She has prepared my body for my burial.'

Jesus knew that soon he would be taken away from his friends and arrested. But his friends did not understand what he meant. Judas was particularly unhappy. He went to find the religious leaders who did not like Jesus. He was ready to agree to betray his friend.

60

Blind Bartimaeus Sees
Luke 18:35-43

Bartimaeus sat by the roadside in Jericho, day after day. He felt the sun warming his skin. He heard the sound of coins being thrown into his begging bowl. He could smell the goat munching on vegetables near to him. But Bartimaeus could not see.

So when Jesus came to Jericho, Bartimaeus wanted to be noticed.

'Jesus, I'm over here!' he called out as he heard a crowd approaching.

Many people wanted to talk to Jesus. He heard the voices of children and the sound of many feet coming closer.

'Jesus, please help me!' he shouted again.

'SShhhh! Jesus is busy,' someone said to him.

But Jesus came towards Bartimaeus.

'What do you want me to do for you?' asked Jesus.

'Please,' begged Bartimaeus, 'I want to be able to see.'

Jesus smiled. He watched as Bartimaeus blinked hard. He saw the huge grin come across his face as he saw the faces of the people all around him.

'Thank you, thank you,' Bartimaeus shouted at the top of his voice. 'I can see! I can see!'

Then Bartimaeus joined the crowd of people who were following Jesus along the road.

Jesus Makes a New Friend
Luke 19:1-9

Zacchaeus was a very SMALL man and a very RICH tax collector. The people of Jericho knew that Zacchaeus cheated them. No one liked him very much.

So when Jesus came to visit, Zacchaeus was keen to see him. If only Jesus could be his friend… But Zacchaeus couldn't even see Jesus over the heads of the people in front.

Zacchaeus decided to climb a fig tree to get a better view. He was just peeping through the branches – when he found the face of Jesus looking up at him! Then, in front of a crowd of people, Jesus asked Zacchaeus if he could come to his house for tea.

Zacchaeus couldn't get down the tree fast enough.

After his meeting with Jesus, Zacchaeus was a new man. 'I want to share what I have with the poor,' he said. 'And if anyone thinks I have cheated them, I will pay them back four times what I owe.'

Jesus smiled. 'This is why I am here,' he said. 'I came to help people who have lost their way.'

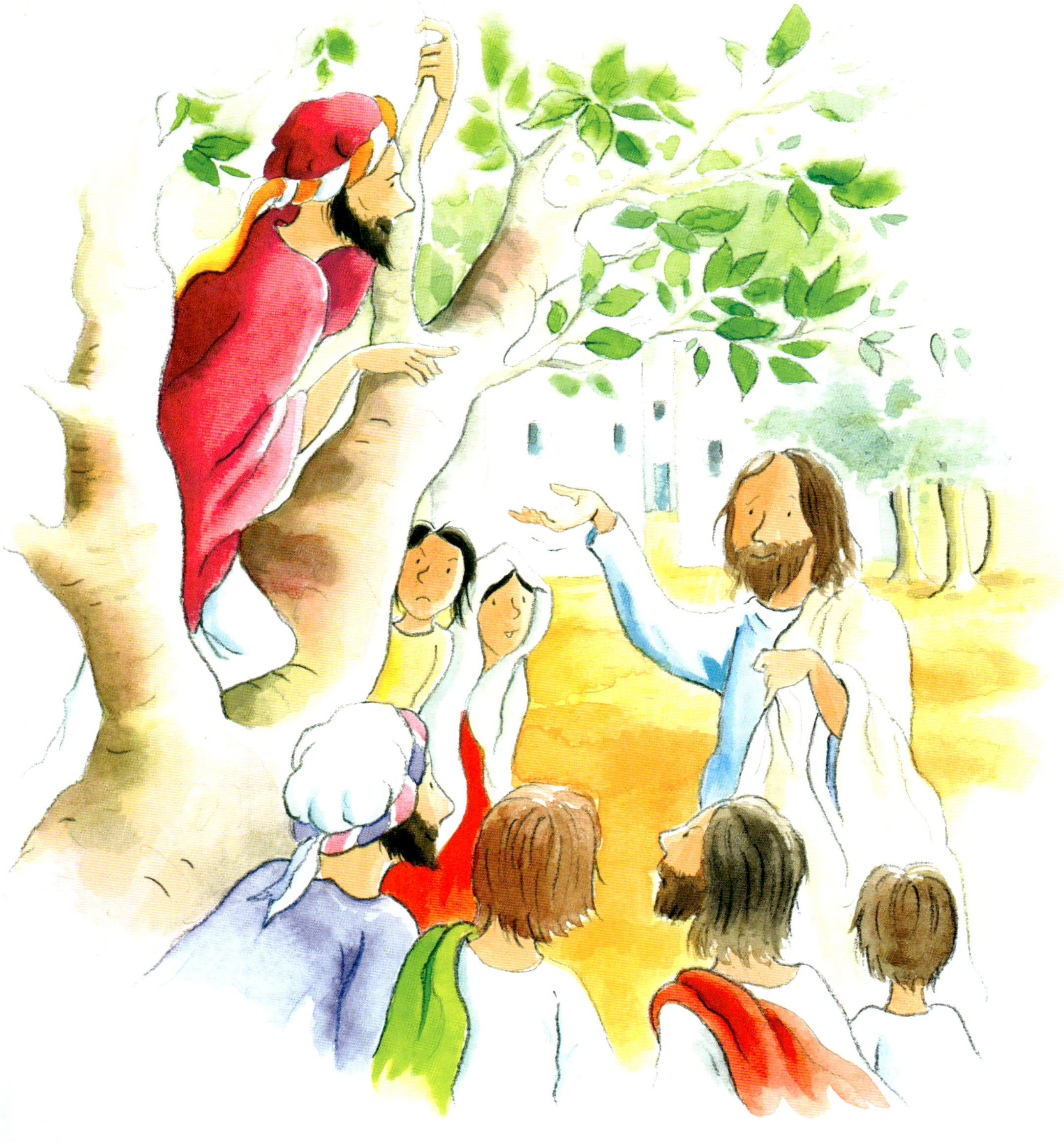

Mary, Martha and Lazarus
John 11:1-46

Jesus often stayed at the home of his friends, Mary, Martha and Lazarus. So when he received a message, telling him that Lazarus was ill, he was very sad.

It was some days before Jesus was able to travel back to visit him. When he approached their home, Martha came out to meet him.

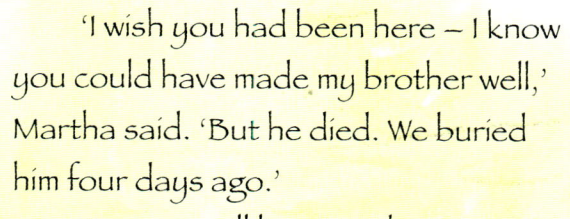

'I wish you had been here – I know you could have made my brother well,' Martha said. 'But he died. We buried him four days ago.'

'Lazarus will live, Martha,' Jesus told her. 'Do you trust me?'

'I know you are God's son,' Martha told him. 'I know you can do anything.'

Mary was inside the house with their friends, weeping for her brother. Martha went to fetch her and they all went to the tomb where Lazarus was buried. Then Jesus was very sad. He cried with them. But Jesus knew what he wanted to do.

'Open the tomb,' he said.

They all watched as the tomb was opened – and Lazarus walked out, no longer dead but alive.

Everyone was happy to have Lazarus back with them. But they were also amazed that Jesus had healed even a dead man. Jesus really was God's son.

Jesus Rides into Jerusalem
Matthew 21:1-11

It was almost the time when everyone celebrated the Passover Feast. Jesus had planned to be with his friends in Jerusalem for the special meal. He knew that he had made some enemies over the past few years: this would be the last time he would be able to do it.

When Jesus reached a village at the Mount of Olives, he asked two of his friends to borrow a donkey from the people there. They spread some clothes over the donkey's back to make it more comfortable, and Jesus climbed on. Then he rode towards the gates of Jerusalem.

There were people lining the streets – men, women and children. Many of them recognized Jesus.

'Here he comes – it's Jesus!'

'Did you hear he healed a blind man?'

'What about the man who couldn't walk – it's a miracle!'

'And he tells wonderful stories!'

The people waved huge palm branches and laid their cloaks down for the donkey to ride over. Everyone was cheering.

'Here comes Jesus!'

'Hooray for Jesus!'

'Praise God – our king is here!'

Some people were less pleased to see the welcome Jesus received.

'Who is this man?' they said. 'Who does he think he is?'

Robbers in the Temple
Luke 19:45-47

The people followed Jesus through the streets of Jerusalem. They followed him into the temple courts. Jesus was going there to pray.

It was not a quiet place. There were people selling doves and pigeons. Others were arguing over the coins they received as the money changers put them into their hands.

'What is happening here?' Jesus asked. 'This is not a market place. It's not a place to buy and sell and cheat people! This is my Father's house and it is a place to pray!'

Jesus tipped over one of the tables. Coins fell everywhere. Birds scattered, squawking.

'Go from here!' Jesus shouted.

Angry men watched as crowds of people came to Jesus to be healed and children danced around him.

The religious leaders saw what had happened. They shook their heads.

'This must stop,' they said to one another. 'We cannot let him stay here any longer.'

'But the people love him and listen to everything he says. We cannot do anything while he is so popular.'

'Then we must find a way. Jesus is not welcome here.'

Living God's Way
Matthew 25:31-46

Over the next few days, Jesus spent time talking with the people who came to him.

'There will come a time when God will say to some of you, "Well done! You were generous with your food and money and shared what you had with me. You took care of me when I was ill and you visited me when I was in prison."

'Don't be surprised! You may not think you did any of those things. But if you ever did this for someone who needed your help, you were doing it for God.'

'But God will say to others, "I am disappointed with you. Why didn't you share your food with me when I was hungry? How could you see me in rags when you had expensive clothes to wear? What were you doing when I was in pain? Where were you when I was lonely in prison?"

'These people will be amazed. They will deny they ever ignored him. But God will say, "I was there every time you did not give money to help someone hungry. I waited in hospital with the person who wanted you to visit. I was always there when you could have helped someone – and you didn't."

'Show God that you love him,' said Jesus. 'Take care of other people. Be kind to anyone who needs your help. God will be there.'

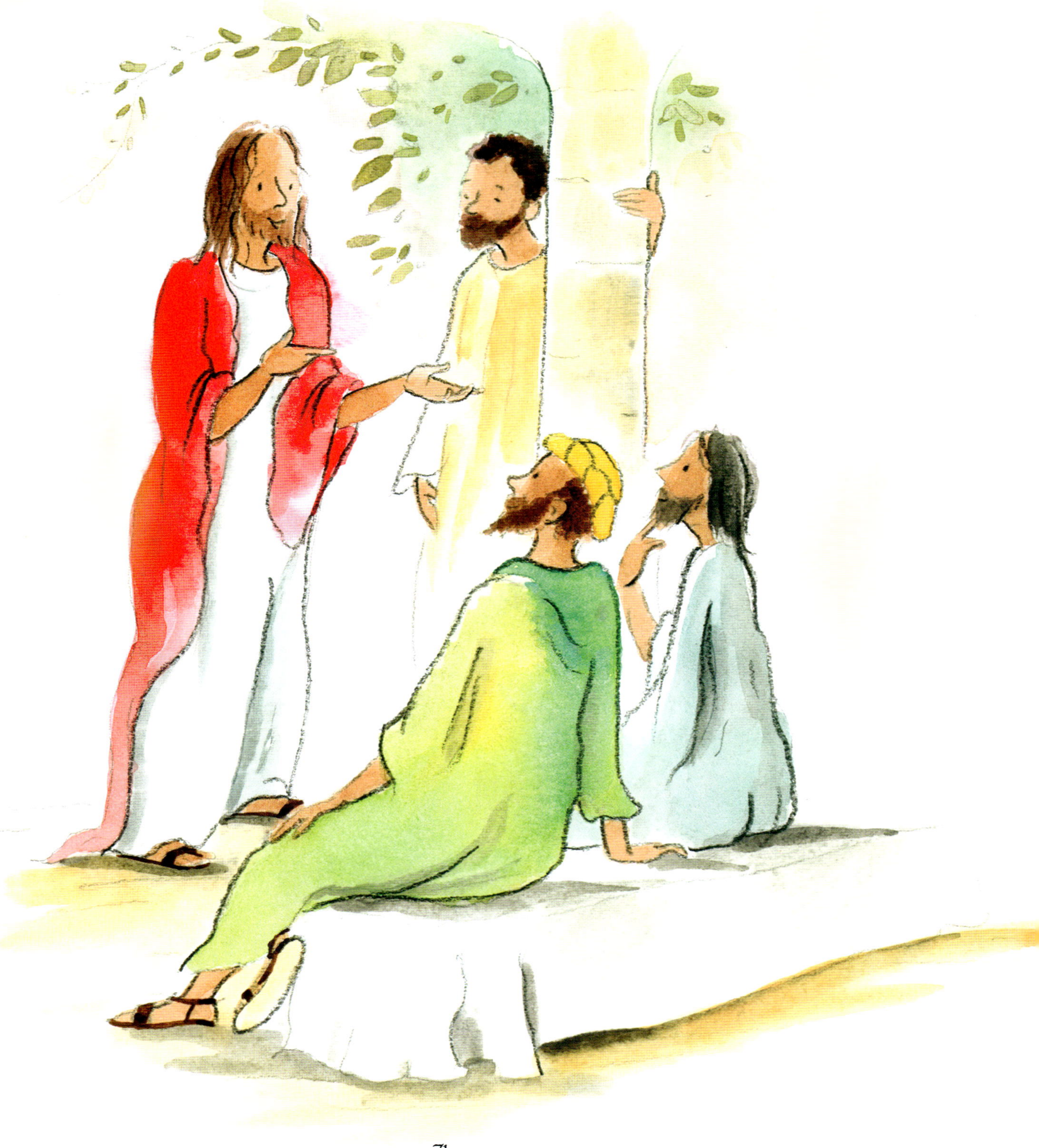

Jesus the Servant
John 13:1-17

On Thursday evening, Jesus and his disciples met together to eat supper in an upstairs room in Jerusalem.

Jesus surprised them by putting a towel around his waist and preparing to wash their dusty feet.

'But this is a servant's job,' said Peter. 'I can't let you wash my feet!'

'That's why I am doing this,' Jesus replied. 'I want to show you that looking after each other in this way is what I want my friends to do. Take care of each other. Treat each other kindly. People will know you are my friends because they will see you are different – you don't think you are too important to wash each other's feet.'

When Jesus had finished, they all settled down to eat. All twelve of Jesus' friends were there.

73

Thirty Pieces of Silver
Luke 22:7-34

Jesus blessed the bread and broke it into pieces. He shared it with friends.

'This is my body,' he said. 'Remember me when you eat together like this. Remember that my body was broken for you.'

Then Jesus blessed the cup of wine and handed it round for each of them to drink.

'This is my blood,' he said. 'Remember me when you drink it. Remember that my blood was shed for you.

'You are all my friends, but one of you will betray me tonight,' Jesus said.

'I would never betray you,' said Peter. 'I would do anything for you!'

'Oh, Peter,' Jesus said sadly, 'before the cock crows tomorrow morning, you will have denied three times that you even know me.'

Judas crept out of the room during the meal. He had already decided to betray Jesus to the religious leaders who hated him. They had given him thirty pieces of silver in exchange for information about where Jesus would be that night.

Soldiers in the Garden
John 18:1-14

Jesus took his friends to a garden of olive trees where he liked to pray. Everyone was tired.

'Stay nearby while I pray,' he told them.

The men sat and watched for a while but soon they fell asleep.

'Father,' Jesus prayed, 'I know what must happen to me. But if there is any other way, please help me now. I want to do what is right. I want to do what you want most of all, but it is so hard.'

When Jesus returned, he found his friends asleep. But he saw that it was already too late.

He could see the light of torches coming towards them in the moonlit garden. Jesus knew that his time with his friends was over.

Judas led a band of men towards him and greeted Jesus with a kiss. It was the sign he had agreed with the soldiers.

Two men came forward and arrested Jesus. Then his friends panicked. Most of them ran away. But as Jesus was led away, Peter and John followed in the shadows, hoping no one would see them.

78

Peter is Ashamed
Matthew 26:57-75

Peter followed Jesus and the men with swords and clubs until Jesus was taken inside. It was dark and cold. He waited in the courtyard, warming his hands by the fire. He tried to understand what was happening. A few hours earlier they had all been eating together. Now – Jesus had been arrested and taken away. But what had he done wrong?

'Aren't you one of Jesus' friends?' someone asked him accusingly.

'No, I don't know him,' Peter said quickly.

'Yes, I'm sure you are,' said another.

'No! Really, I don't know him!' Peter said again.

A while later, just as it was beginning to get light, someone else spoke to Peter.

'You have the same accent – from Galilee.'

'I told you! I don't know Jesus!'

Jesus was still inside the building. They had been asking him questions all night. At that moment Jesus turned and saw Peter outside.

Then a cock crowed. It was morning.

The Crown of Thorns
Matthew 27:11-31

The Jewish leaders took Jesus to Pontius Pilate. They wanted him to be executed. They needed the Roman governor for that.

Pilate questioned Jesus too. He knew the people loved him. Nothing Jesus said seemed to be a crime. Even the Roman governor needed a reason to have some one executed.

Pilate took Jesus outside and showed him to the people.

'Look! Here is Jesus, the man some of you call a king. I can't find him guilty of any crime. But it is the custom to release a prisoner at this time of year. Shall I release Jesus? Or would you prefer the murderer, Barabbas?'

Pilate expected the people to ask for Jesus – he could set him free and the religious leaders could do nothing. But Jesus' enemies were prepared. They had people in the crowd ready for this moment.

'Barabbas!' they shouted. 'We want Barabbas!'

'But what shall I do with Jesus?' asked Pilate.

'Crucify him!' they shouted even louder. 'Crucify him!'

Pilate washed his hands. He would not be guilty of this innocent man's murder.

'Take him away,' he ordered the soldiers.

The soldiers put a crown made out of thorns on his head and dressed him in a purple robe. They whipped him. When he was weak and tired, they led him away to be crucified.

80

81

The Three Crosses
John 19:17-42

Jesus carried the heavy wooden cross on which he would be crucified on his shoulder. He stumbled along the street watched by weeping women and children.

When they reached the place of execution, on a hill called Golgotha, the soldiers put him on the cross between two criminals.

'I thought you were God's son,' said one. 'If you are – save yourself and us too!'

'We deserve our punishment,' said the other. 'He's done nothing wrong. Remember me when you get to heaven, Jesus.'

'Today you will be with me in Paradise,' Jesus replied.

Mary, his mother, was there weeping. John, one of his friends was there comforting her.

'Look after her, John,' Jesus told him. 'Treat her as your own mother.'

'This is your son, now, Mother,' Jesus said to Mary. 'He will look after you.'

Many people cried as they saw how Jesus suffered on the cross. This was the man who had healed people, the man who was their friend. How could this have happened?

As the hours passed, the sky grew dark.

Finally Jesus spoke one last time before he died.

'It is finished!'

A soldier stood nearby.

'This really was God's son!' he said.

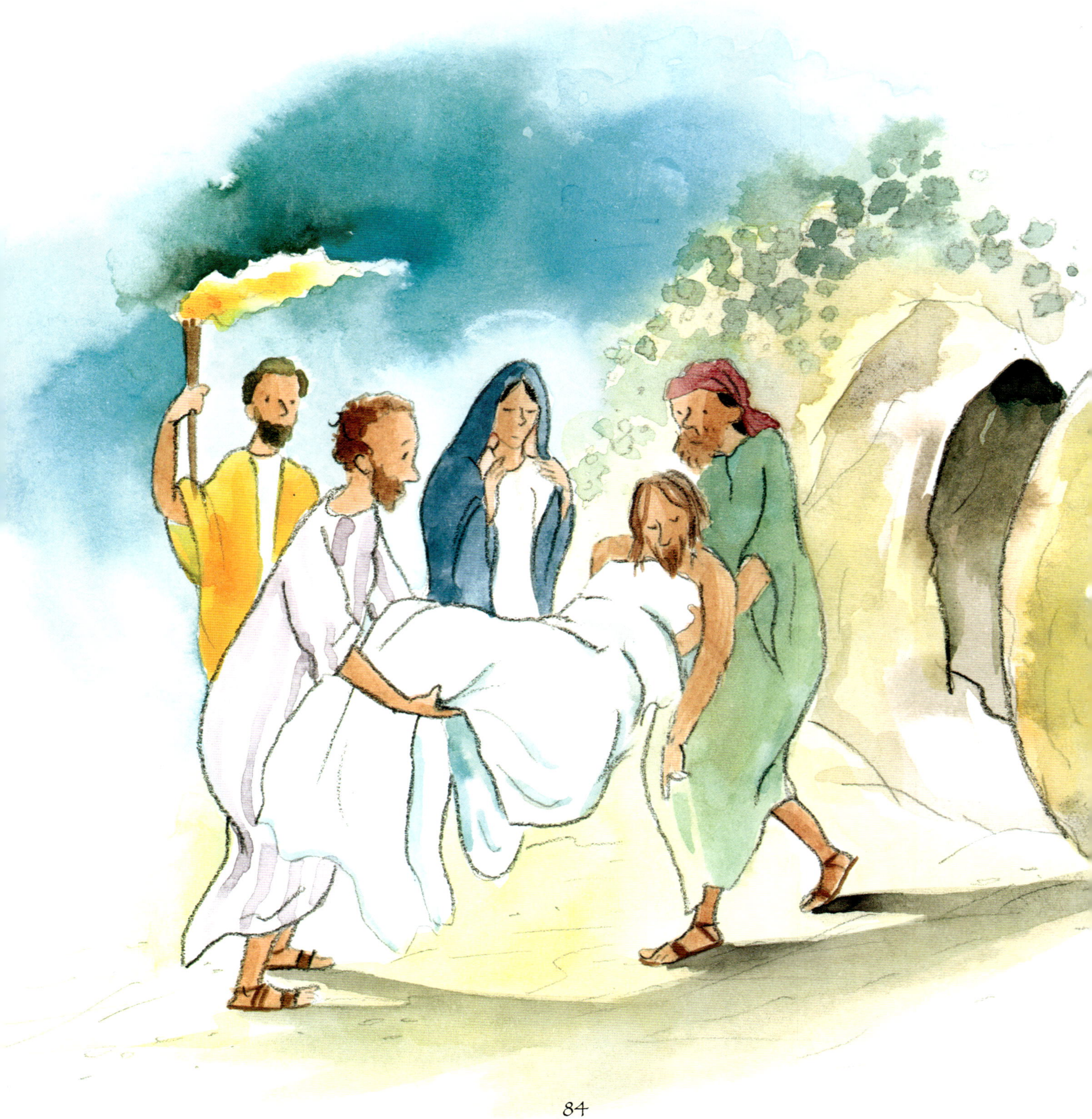

Jesus is Buried
Matthew 27:57-61

That evening, a rich man called Joseph, who came from Arimathea, went to visit Pontius Pilate. He had met Jesus and heard the things he told people about God. He had become one of Jesus' friends.

Joseph did not want Jesus' body left on the cross. He asked for permission to take it down and bury it properly in the tomb he had prepared for his own burial one day.

The Roman governor gave him permission. Joseph went with another friend and took down the body. They wrapped it in a clean linen cloth, and placed it in the rock tomb in a garden. They rolled a large stone door in front of the entrance of the tomb before sunset the same day.

Mary Magdalene and some of the other women followed them. They wanted to see where they had put the body of their friend.

The Empty Tomb
Luke 24:1-12

Mary Magdalene woke before dawn on Sunday morning. She gathered some herbs and spices in a basket and went with the other women to the tomb where she had seen the men bury Jesus.

When they arrived in the garden, the first thing they saw was the large stone rolled away from the entrance. They went nearer and looked inside. The tomb was empty!

'Why are you looking here for a dead man? Don't you know that Jesus is alive!' It was the voice of an angel.

The women ran back to the town to find the disciples. They found the eleven friends and told them that the tomb was empty. Jesus had risen from the dead!

The men did not believe them. Peter and John ran back to the tomb to see for themselves. They also saw the stone rolled away and the linen that had wrapped the body still in the tomb. But Jesus was not there. What could have happened?

87

Thomas Believes
John 20:24-28

That evening, the friends talked together behind locked doors about what had happened. They were still frightened that soldiers would come for them too.

Suddenly Jesus appeared in the room with them. He had not unlocked or opened the door – but he was there and he was very much alive! He showed them the wounds in his hands and his side and talked with them for a while.

Thomas had not been there when Jesus came to the locked room.

'Unless I see Jesus for myself and touch his wounds – I just can't believe it!' he said when they told him.

Jesus came again to the locked room about a week later.

Thomas was amazed!

'Hello, Thomas,' said Jesus. 'Touch my hands. Can you believe now that I am here and not a dead man?'

Thomas did not need to touch him. He fell to his knees.

'It is you, Lord! I do believe.'

'I am glad you can believe what you see with your own eyes,' said Jesus. 'But many will be blessed in the future when they believe what has happened even though they have not seen me.'

Breakfast by the Lake
John 21:1-14

The disciples went back to Galilee after a while. One night Peter asked if anyone wanted to go fishing.

Seven of the friends went out on the lake. They were out all night but caught nothing. Then as the sun rose they heard someone calling to them from the shore.

'Let down your nets on the other side of the boat,' the man said.

The fishermen put down their nets again – and caught so many fish that the nets nearly broke.

They knew who the man on the shore must be.

'It's Jesus!' one of them shouted.

Peter could not wait for the boat to come to shore. He jumped overboard and waded through the water.

Jesus was warming some bread over a small fire.

'Bring some fish and we can have breakfast,' he said.

Peter was anxious about being with Jesus. He still felt bad about telling people that he was not his friend.

'Do you love me, Peter?' Jesus asked him. He asked him three times.

'You know I do!' replied Peter.

'I want you to look after all my friends, Peter. Take good care of them.'

Jesus Returns to Heaven
Acts 1:1-11

Jesus met his friends from time to time for forty days after his resurrection. They never knew when or where they would see him. But Jesus ate with them and talked with them.

The eleven disciples and the women were not the only people to see him. Sometimes he came and talked to a whole crowd of the people who had been his friends.

There was one more important thing he had to tell them.

'Stay in Jerusalem,' he said. 'Wait for the gift of the Holy Spirit to be given to you. Then God will give you the power

to tell everyone you meet about what
I have taught you about God. Tell
them how I died and about the miracle of the
resurrection. Tell everyone. Make sure people all
over the world know what you know. I will always be
there to help you.'

Then Jesus left them for the last time. A cloud hid him and he returned to God, his father, in heaven.

Angels appeared just afterwards.

'He has gone now,' the angels said. 'But he'll come back one day. It will be just as amazing!'